Remembering
Denver

T0122471

Myron Vallier

TURNER
PUBLISHING COMPANY

This view of downtown Denver taken in 1909, shows the Arapahoe County Court House on the left and the Majestic Building near the start of 16th Street. The Front Range is in the distance.

Contents

The Brown Palace Hotel, located at the intersection of Broadway and Tremont Place, was designed by Frank E. Edbrooke, for Henry C. Brown, and opened in 1892. It is still one of the great hotels of the world.

ACKNOWLEDGMENTS

This volume, *Remembering Denver,* is the result of the cooperation and efforts of many individuals and organizations. It takes a community to preserve local history, especially visual history. The photographs featured in this book come from the Denver Public Library Western History/Genealogy Department's Western History Photograph Collection. This archive contains more than 600,000 photographs and negatives that document the history of Colorado and the trans-Mississippi West.

The library's photo database contains more than 110,000 images and catalog records of North American Indians, pioneer life, railroads, mining, Denver, Colorado towns, city, farm, and ranch life, recreation, landscape, as well as numerous other subjects.

Most of the digitized material on the Web site is from the Denver Public Library's Western History Photograph Collection; however, there is also a significant amount of material from the Colorado Historical Society photograph collection. The library sells high-resolution photographic prints, transparencies, and digital files of any of Denver Public Library's images on the Web site. To view or find more information about the collection or to order images, visit the library's Web site at

www.photoswest.org

This volume would not have been possible without the professional and amateur historians devoted to preserving the past, including the dedicated staff—past and present—of the Denver Public Library.

Coi Drummond-Gehrig
Linda Running Bently
Bruce Hanson

The publisher would also like to thank Myron Vallier, the writer, for his valuable contributions and assistance in making this work possible.

PREFACE

Denver has thousands of historic photographs that reside in archives, both locally and nationally. This book began with the observation that, while those photographs are of great interest to many, they are not easily accessible. During a time when Denver is looking ahead and evaluating its future course, many people are asking, How do we treat the past? These decisions affect every aspect of the city—architecture, public spaces, commerce, infrastructure—and these, in turn, affect the way that people live their lives. This book seeks to provide easy access to a valuable, objective look into the history of Denver.

The power of photographs is that they are less subjective than words in their treatment of history. Although the photographer can make subjective decisions regarding subject matter and how to capture and present it, photographs seldom interpret the past to the extent textual histories can. For this reason, photography is uniquely positioned to offer an original, untainted look at the past, allowing the viewer to learn for himself what the world was like a century or more ago.

This project represents countless hours of review and research. The researchers and writer have reviewed thousands of photographs in numerous archives. We greatly appreciate the generous assistance of those listed in the acknowledgments of this work, without whom this project could not have been completed.

The goal in publishing this work is to provide broader access to this set of extraordinary photographs which seek to inspire, provide perspective, and evoke insight that might assist people who are responsible for determining Denver's future. In addition, the book seeks to preserve the past with adequate respect and reverence.

With the exception of touching up imperfections that have accrued with the passage of time and cropping where necessary, no changes have been made. The focus and clarity of many images are limited to the technology and the ability of the photographer at the time they were recorded.

The work is divided into eras. Beginning with some of the earliest known photographs of Denver, the first section records photographs from the Civil War era through the late nineteenth century. The second section spans the early years of the twentieth century through the World War I era. Section Three moves to the twenties and thirties, and the last section covers the World War II era.

In each of these sections we have made an effort to capture various aspects of life through our selection of photographs. People, commerce, transportation, infrastructure, religious institutions, and educational institutions have been included to provide a broad perspective.

We encourage readers to reflect as they go walking in Denver, strolling through the city, its parks, and its neighborhoods. It is the publisher's hope that in utilizing this work, longtime residents will learn something new and that new residents will gain a perspective on where Denver has been, so that each can contribute to its future.

—Todd Bottorff, Publisher

Denver newspaper police reporters pose in front of the old Denver City Hall. The men are identified as George Flanagan and Mudge Ransom, in the front row, and George Minot, Walter Lovelace, an unidentified reporter, Johnny Day, and Joe Satterthwaite, in the back row.

Becoming "Queen City of the Plains"
(1858–1899)

The Rocky Mountain News office, built in 1860, was destroyed by the Cherry Creek flood in 1864.
The newspaper, founded by William Newton Byers, is still in existence.

The early city of Denver suffered great damage, and the city of Auraria was wiped out, when Cherry Creek flooded in 1864. Despite warnings of the potential hazard, the settlers had built near the river. Here we see well-dressed residents surveying the damage from both sides of the creek.

City policemen dressed in uniform and young boys pose in front of the City Jail located in the former Butterick Meat Market building at 1355 13th Street. One of Denver's earliest jails, it was located here from 1866 through 1883.

The Denver City Home Guard was organized in 1861 to fight in the Civil War and attached to the District of Colorado. The guard marched to New Mexico and engaged Confederate troops on February 21, 1862, at Valverde, south of Socorro. The guard was mustered out on April 1, 1862.

Originally the U.S. Branch Mint, located near the corner of 16th and Holladay (later Market) streets, was the Clark, Gruber & Company bank and mint. The business was sold to the government in 1863. The original building was then incorporated into the building shown here.

Covered wagons crowd 15th Street in this photograph taken in 1865. The photographic studio of William G. Chamberlain is on the corner of Larimer Street.

A view of 15th Street in the 1860s. The Filmore Block is on the corner.

The First National Bank building on the corner of 15th and Blake streets was built in the mid-1860s. The third story was added in the early 1870s. The building was the site of the Colorado Constitutional Convention held between December 1875 and March 1876.

The Duhem Brothers, noted Denver photographers, had a studio located at 448 Larimer Street. The carriage parked in front of the building at right holds a portable darkroom.

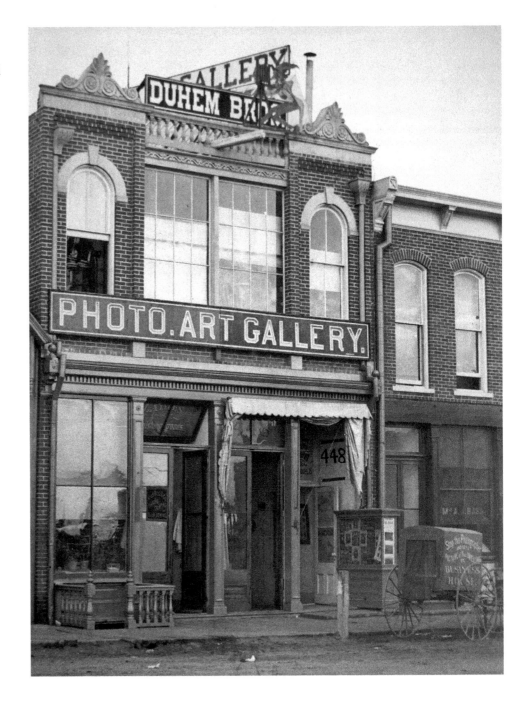

A view of Wolfe Hall, an Episcopalian women's seminary school at 17th and Champa streets. Built in 1867, this was one of Denver's earliest private schools. It was founded by Denver's first Episcopal Bishop, George Randall.

Central Denver was rapidly changing by the middle of the 1870s. Arapahoe School, built in 1872, was Denver's first public school; it is shown in the center of this image with a tile roof and cupola. By 1882, the area had been engulfed by the city's growing business district, and the school was closed.

The Inter-Ocean Hotel built by Barney Frank, an African-American entrepreneur, opened on October 29, 1873, and was one of the city's leading hotels. It was located at the corner of 16th and Blake streets.

Located on the corner of 17th and Lawrence, the Grand Central Hotel opened in 1872. After being sold in 1882 and extensively remodeled, the enlarged facility reopened as the Markham Hotel.

The First Baptist Church of Denver was established in 1864 and is the oldest Baptist Congregation in Denver and Colorado. The original building, shown here, was built in 1873 at the corner of Larimer and 15th streets.

The first Daniels and Fisher store was located at 390 Larimer Street. It became Denver's premier department store and lasted well into the twentieth century.

A Chinese band leads a funeral procession near Hop Alley, a neighborhood of Chinese laborers settled in 1870 by laid-off railroad workers. The area was located between Blake and Wazee streets near 20th Street. In 1880, an anti-Chinese riot started in Hop Alley and much of the area was destroyed.

This bird's-eye view of Denver, taken in the early 1880s, is dominated by the Episcopal Cathedral of Saint John the Evangelist. The church was located on the corner of 20th and Welton streets.

Bartenders stand on the steps of the Beer Depot of the Union Brewing Company located at 2433 Sixteenth Street in Denver, Colorado. Waiters pose next door at the Depot Restaurant. In 1900, the Union Brewery merged with the Tivoli Brewing Company to form the Tivoli Union Brewing Company, which remained in business until 1969.

Horse-drawn carriages, wagons, and delivery vans crowd the intersection of 16th Street and Arapahoe Street. The Union Bank, a three-story stone building, is on the corner. Well-dressed men and women sport umbrellas to shade themselves from the sun.

A view of the Italianate McClintock Block located on the corner of 16th and Larimer streets. The Dewey Hotel, an eight-story stone building, is next door. Denver Tramway trolley cars travel down Larimer Street.

The Tabor Opera House, designed by Frank E. and Willoughby J. Edbrooke, was built by silver magnate Horace A. W. Tabor at a cost of more than $850,000. Opening in 1881, it was one of the most ornate and magnificent structures west of the Mississippi. Tabor would meet Elizabeth Bonduel McCourt in 1880. Although he was married to Augusta Tabor, he and "Baby Doe" would begin a liaison that would eventually lead to his divorce. After their marriage, Tabor lost his considerable fortune in the silver crash of 1893. He died in 1899 leaving his wife and children impoverished. Baby Doe would die in 1935 frozen to the floor of a cabin at a former Tabor mine, the Matchless.

The Arapahoe County courthouse, built in 1883, was located at 16th and Tremont streets. Originally, Denver was part of Arapahoe County. When the City and County of Denver were incorporated in 1902, it became the Denver County Courthouse. It remained in use until the early 1930s when it was demolished.

This 1884 view of a thriving Larimer Street reflects the city's growth driven by mining and railroads. During the 1880s Denver's population of 106,000 people made it the second-largest city in the West.

This view of the old United States Post Office located at 16th and Arapahoe streets was inadequate for postal services when it opened in the 1880s. A new post office was built in 1916, and this building served as the U.S. Customs House until it was demolished in 1965.

This panorama of 17th Street shows how the city prospered during the boom of the 1880s. The large Renaissance Revival building in the distance is the Equitable Building, Denver's first high rise when it was completed in 1892, just before the depression of 1893.

Members of a tennis club pose on a tennis court in front of their clubhouse. Florence Ward (Holland) wears a dress with a light bodice and striped skirt and holds a tennis racket. Edward Wolcott, later U.S. senator from Colorado, stands at the extreme right.

A view of the old City Hall located at 14th Street and Larimer. The stone and granite building was built in 1886 and was later used by the fire department and the police department before being razed in 1945.

This view of Stout Street shows how the commercial heart of Denver was beginning to grow in the 1880s and 1890s. The building on the left houses the Women's Exchange, a benevolent organization for needy women. The First Baptist Church is visible in the distance.

Ute Indians camp at the 1884 National Mining and Industrial Exposition. The building in view in the background, located in South Denver just East of Broadway, was built specifically to house expositions. The 1884 exposition, however, turned out to be a financial failure and it was discontinued. The building was sold and later razed.

This French Chateau–style house was designed by architect Theodore Davis Boal, for Captain Decatur Bethel. It was located at the corner of Colfax Avenue and Marion Street.

Denver City Cable Railway Company cable car number 31 is stopped near the corner of 15th Street and Lawrence in the Central Business District. The seven street-railway cables extended over nearly 30 miles and were powered by a single power plant.

The Denver Club, a private men's club, was organized in 1880 by some of the city's most illustrious civic leaders, including David Moffat, Walter Cheesman, and Henry Wolcott. The Victorian Romanesque–style building, designed by Frederick Junius Sterner, opened in 1888 and continued in use until 1953. The First Congregational Church is next door.

Wolfe Hall, an Episcopalian seminary for young ladies, was located between 13th and 14th avenues on Clarkson Street. The school moved to this building, designed by John W. Roberts, in 1889. The chateau-style building was razed in 1920.

The railroad Gothic-style Union Depot opened in 1881.

Horse-drawn wagons are parked on both sides of North Lawrence in the Central Business District in the mid-1880s. A large incandescent streetlight hangs in the intersection of 15th and Lawrence streets.

Early in the 1890s these men pose in front of the Scandinavian Saloon at 1719 Blake Street. The bartender stands in the center of the group in a white coat and apron. A pair of safety bicycles are parked behind the two men at left.

Following the depression of 1893, Ohio businessman Jacob Coxey organized an "Industrial Army" of the unemployed. "Coxey's Army" was created to protest the government's failure to deal with the economic crisis. In this picture, probably from 1894, unemployed men stand near boats that they have built near Riverside Park. They are preparing for a journey over water and land to attend a demonstration organized by Coxey in Washington, D.C. The park's racecourse grandstand is visible in the distance.

Men pose on and near a streetcar and an observation car at the corner of Colorado Avenue and South Broadway on the newly constructed South Denver Cable Railway Line on December 25, 1889. The electric streetcar service began in January 1890.

Members of the First Colorado Infantry Volunteers ride past City Hall bound for the Philippines in the Spanish-American War. The horse-drawn wagons carry cannon and soldiers.

The Romanesque Revival–style Masonic Building located at 16th and Welton streets was built in 1890 by F. E. Edbrooke & Company. For many years it served as the center for the activities of the Masonic Order in Colorado. The bottom floors were rented out for business.

Members of the Colorado Infantry stand in formation on Lawrence Street during the "City Hall War," a dispute between Governor Davis Waite and two of his appointees to Denver's police and fire boards. Waite attempted to forcibly remove these men as well as some of his other appointees from office. When City Hall employees learned of this, they barricaded themselves inside City Hall. The entire Denver police department and many sheriffs' deputies were later to join them outside the building. Finally the court ordered board members to give up their seats, but ruled that the governor had exceeded his authority in calling out the infantry.

The Italian Renaissance–style Equitable Building, built by the Equitable Life Insurance Company, was located at 17th and Stout streets. It was Denver's first high rise when completed in 1892.

This man in his suit and top hat rides a bicycle adapted as a velocipede for the tracks in the railroad yards near 20th Street.

Turner Moving & Storage Company horse-drawn moving vans are lined up on 16th Street in front of the Denver Republican Newspaper building. The large merchant wagons are pulled by four-horse teams.

The Manhattan Beach amusement park, located on the northwestern shore of Sloan's Lake, opened in 1891. The park featured a summer stock theater and a large roller coaster. In 1906, a fire destroyed the theater; soon after the park's steamboat, *City of Denver,* sank. The Manhattan Beach park closed and was reopened as Luna Park.

The Ernest & Cranmer Building was located at 17th and Curtis streets. Designed by architect Frank E. Edbrooke and Company, it opened in 1891. The first two floors of the building were constructed using Colorado red sandstone; the upper part was built of brown brick.

Gentlemen rest in the lobby of the Brown Palace Hotel, lavishly appointed with velvet upholstered furniture with brass ball feet. The eight-story atrium has pillars, elaborate pierced brass railings, and wainscoting of pale golden onyx. Discreetly placed spittoons are scattered about the room.

This 1892 Romanesque Revival–style church was designed by Denver architects Frank Edbrooke and Willis Marean. It is located on the corner of 17th and Sherman streets. The Colorado state capitol is visible in the distance.

The Cathedral of Saint John the Evangelist was the first Episcopal cathedral in Colorado. Located on the corner of 20th and Welton streets, it opened in 1881. It was destroyed by fire in 1903.

People gather in front of the 1896 Spanish Revival–style City Park pavilion to listen to a band concert on the shore of Lake Ferril. Band members sit in the bandstand located in the manmade lake.

In this view of Union Station, rebuilt after the 1894 fire, a trolley takes on passengers near the Oxford Hotel built in 1891 by Frank Edbrooke. Union Station was rebuilt again in 1912 with the central section becoming today's Union Station.

Spectators crowd bleachers set up in front of the Colorado state capitol to watch a parade at the Festival of Mountain and Plain. Ute Indians ride their horses past the grandstands.

The Hotel Metropole opened in 1891, located at 18th Avenue and Broadway. The building housed
the well-known Broadway Theatre. In 1926 the building was combined
with, and incorporated into, the Cosmopolitan Hotel.

This barbecue at the Denver Union Stock Yards was probably held as a promotional event for the play "Shall We Forgive Her" by Frank Harvey. Women prepare slabs of meat for the well-dressed crowd. Posters in the Distance read "Shall We Forgive Her."

Constructed by the Youngstown Bridge Company at a cost of $367,068, the 14th Street Viaduct was a joint project of the cities of Denver and Highlands (later incorporated into Denver). The bridge had 63 spans and totaled 1,467 feet in length. It was built to carry wagons, streetcars, and pedestrians across the South Platte River.

In this image, a bartender, waiters, and customers pose in a bar in Denver.

The Chamberlin Observatory at the University of Denver was designed by Robert S. Roeschlaub and built in 1890. It houses the famous 20-inch Alvan Clark-Saegmuller refractor telescope still in use today.

The Iliff School of Theology opened as a department of the University of Denver in 1892. It closed temporarily in the early twentieth century before reopening as an independent institution in 1910.

In this view of Denver, 16th Street is in the center of the picture. On the left is the Arapahoe County Courthouse and on the right is the Majestic Building. Behind that is the Kittredge Building. Visible in the distance is the front range of the Rockies.

BIRTH OF THE CITY BEAUTIFUL
(1900–1919)

The Gano Clothing Company, one of Denver's finest men's stores, did business in the Steele Building located at the corner of 16th and Stout streets.

British golfer Harry Vardon was one of golf's first international superstars. He is shown here at the Overland Country Club golf course in December 1900 during an exhibition tour.

The cornerstone for the Denver City Auditorium was laid in September 1907 and the building was dedicated June 1, 1908. Mayor Speer and the Denver Chamber of Commerce raised $100,000 to celebrate both the opening of the new building and the Democratic National Convention, Denver's only national political convention.

Wagons filled with snow from Rollins Pass are on display on 15th Street probably during the 1908 Democratic Convention. The snow came from the Denver, Northwestern, and Pacific Railway's Moffat Road, the highest railroad line ever built in the United States.

A Denver policeman detains an intoxicated man in front of a "drunk tank" on Larimer Street in 1905.

The Daniels and Fisher Department Store was one of the city's finest retail establishments for many years. In this photograph, men on horseback ride down 16th Street past the department store, which has an enormous United States flag draped across its facade.

Members of the Daniels and Fisher cadets, composed of "cash boys," train on the roof of the store. Cash boys carried a customer's merchandise and cash to an "inspector" and returned with the wrapped merchandise and the customer's change.

The Hayden, Dickinson, & Feldhauser building was built in 1891 as a retail building and then expanded in 1909 when several more floors were added. It was later renamed the Colorado Building and in 1937 it was given an Art Deco facade.

The White City, an amusement park, was inaugurated by Mayor Robert Speer in 1908. This view is from atop the "Big Splash." The park, located right outside the city limits, was a favorite of Denver residents. It was later renamed Lakeside Amusement Park and is still in operation today.

In this photograph taken in 1912 or later, veteran members of the Rough Riders, the First U.S. Volunteer Cavalry Regiment during the Spanish-American War, ride through the Welcome Arch in front of Union Station. The Welcome or Mizpah Arch was dedicated July 4, 1906. Illuminated with 1,600 light bulbs, it weighed more than 70 tons. The arch was removed in 1931 because it was considered a traffic hazard.

With students dressed as clowns, the teacher's baseball team poses for the camera at Manual Training
High School located at 27th and Franklin streets.

Well-dressed men and women sit in an open tour bus in City Park.

President Theodore Roosevelt rides down 17th Street in an open car during his visit to Denver. A secret service agent is kneeling on the running board of the automobile. During this visit the president delivered a speech to the Colorado Stock Association titled "Conservation." Union Station is visible in the distance.

Located at the corner of 17th and Stout streets, the Italianate Albany Hotel opened in 1885. After several sweeping renovations and a catastrophic fire, it was finally demolished in 1977.

This round-about was located at the intersection of 16th Street and Broadway in the Central Business District. In the distance, the State Capitol dome rises behind the Plymouth Hotel.

The Nast Photo studio was located on the corner of 11th and Curtis streets. Nast was one of Denver's pioneer photographers. Arriving in Denver in 1875, he worked as a reporter for the *Denver Tribune,* and was active as a photographer from 1880 to 1901. The Scholtz Drug Company was located below the Nast Studio and the Majestic Theater.

Here a Denver police officer operates a portable traffic signal at an intersection in the Central Business District.

Two women in wet bathing suits and caps walk along the edge of Smith Lake in Washington Park. Many of the women spectators hold umbrellas to shield themselves from the sun.

Horse-drawn wagons filled with snow line 16th Street after the great blizzard of 1913, in which 36 inches of snow brought the city to a standstill. The snow was carted to Civic Center where it was piled in front of the State Capitol.

This view shows turn-of-the-century 16th Street filled with pedestrians, horse-drawn wagons and carriages, automobiles, and an electric streetcar. The Capitol is visible in the distance.

Plainclothes policemen escort a handcuffed prisoner out of Union Station.

The Mining Exchange Building located on the corner of 15th and Arapahoe streets opened in 1891 to become the financial center for the mining industry in the Rocky Mountain West. In 1963, the structure was razed to make way for a modern office building. The *Old Prospector,* the statue mounted on top of the building, was saved and is now on display in front of Brooks Towers on 15th Street between Curtis and Arapahoe.

President William Howard Taft visited Denver on October 3, 1911. The president came to the city to address the Public Lands Convention.

The Princess Theatre in view here was located at 1620 Curtis Street.

A Benedict Transfer and Storage Company horse-drawn wagon is parked near the company's office in the 1500 block of Glenarm Place.

The J. P. Fink's Block was located on the corner of 15th and Market streets. When it was erected in 1873 it was considered one of the city's finest buildings.

Curtis Street, known as Theater Row, was home to many of Denver's most illustrious movie theaters. This 1913 view shows the Iris, Isis, Princess, Empress, and Tabor Grand theaters.

Policemen on horseback hold back a throng of spectators at a foot race on Champa Street. The Denver Post building is on the left; a close look reveals an electric baseball scoreboard over the front door.

Members of the Denver police department mounted patrol pose on horseback in front of the Denver County jail, located at Colfax and Santa Fe avenues.

This man in dirty overalls and a hat poses next to a touring car in City Park. An elderly woman in the backseat has on a touring hat and goggles.

In this harness race at City Park, sulkies pass the covered grandstand and spectators watch from a tour bus parked beside the track. The racetrack was built in 1898 and was finally razed in 1950.

Sailors and soldiers gather around a piano at a Red Cross canteen.

In 1917, recruits for World War I ride in a parade in Denver. Men on a car carry a sign taking a poke at Germany's Kaiser; a dead duck hangs from the sign. Another sign reads "Their jobs are waiting."

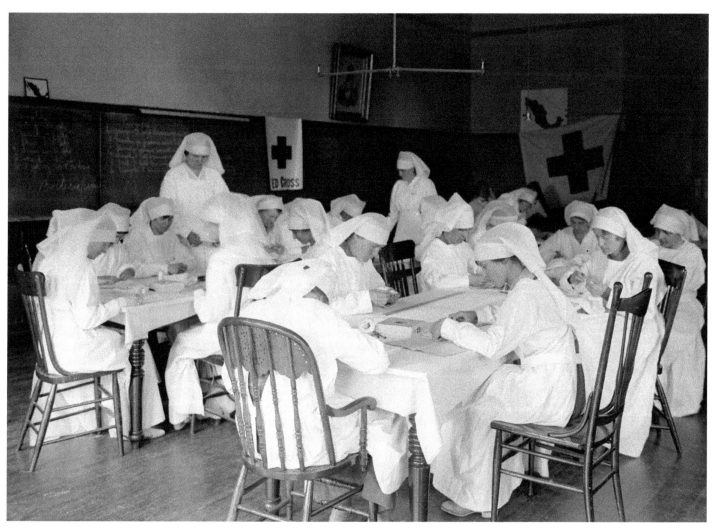

Red Cross nurses at Loretto Heights College teach first aid trainees how to roll bandages for the World War I war effort.

Recruits depart from Fort Logan, a military training camp in Denver. The troops wait to board
Denver and Rio Grande Western Railroad cars.

Ushers for the Broadway Theater pose in front of the entrance at 1756 Broadway. The theater was part of the Metropole Hotel and was for years one of Denver's finest movie houses. One of the ushers wears an Army uniform.

Rocky Mountain Park was another of the parks created during the Speer administration. Located in the Berkeley neighborhood, it was established in 1906.

Progress, Depression, and New Deal
(1920–1939)

Boxer Jack Dempsey and his wife, actress Estelle Taylor, pose in front of their train at Union Station. Dempsey was born in Manassa, Colorado, in 1895, earning legendary status as a champion heavyweight boxer.

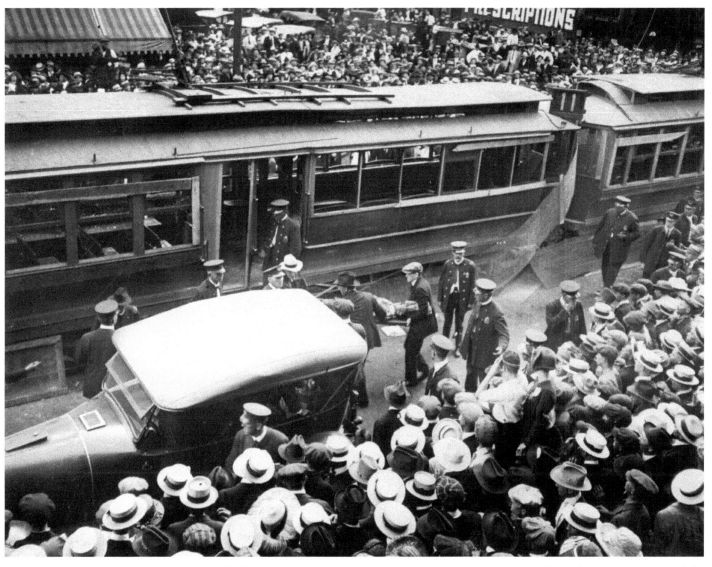

On the first of August 1920, the Denver Tramway employees union declared a strike over wages. The company hired a professional strikebreaker, John C. "Black Jack" Jerome, to attempt to restart streetcar service. Several violent clashes broke out between the strikers and the strikebreakers. Days later the strike culminated in a riot, streetcars were damaged and overturned, and streetcar barns were burned. Eventually federal troops from Fort Logan and Camp Funston, Kansas, were brought in to quell the strike, but not before six people had been killed.

Denver's "Auto Bandit Chaser" was designed by the Denver police department. The specially equipped vehicle was armor-plated and had a mounted machine gun, siren, and bell. The vehicle was in service for a very short time in 1921 before it overturned in an accident. The "Bandit Chaser" was never repaired.

The Romanesque Revival Holy Rosary Church, designed by Denver architect L. A. Desjardins, is located at 4695 Pearl Street in the Globeville neighborhood. The church played an important role in the lives of the Slovenian and Croatian members of the parish.

Two couples sit in the "Wildcat," a traditional camelback wooden roller coaster in Elitch Gardens, which was located at 4620 West 38th Avenue. Elitch's, opened by John and Mary Elitch in 1890, was on the site of Chilcott Farm. The park grew to include beautiful gardens, the Trocadero ballroom, a zoo, a summer stock theater, and a wide variety of amusement rides. The park was closed in 1994.

By the 1920s Denver had become the leading livestock market west of the Missouri River. It was home to five leading packing plants and numerous slaughterhouses. This interior shot shows men removing the hides from cattle carcasses.

People sit on wire benches in the Voorhies Memorial pergola in Civic Center. The memorial, inspired by the Water Gateway at the 1893 Columbian Exposition, was designed by Fisher and Fisher Architects and completed in 1919. Allen True, a well-known Colorado painter, created silhouette buffaloes and elk in the Greek style for the lunettes of the arches in the memorial. The State Capitol is visible in the distance.

Cheesman Park is located on a hill overlooking the Front Range. Originally Mt. Prospect Cemetery, in 1890 it was discovered that the land had originally been Indian land ceded to the government by treaty. The government then sold the land to Denver, and the cemetery was renamed Denver City Cemetery. The following year the city decided to vacate the cemetery. This resulted in a major scandal. Corrupt officials allowed haphazard removal of bodies, and as a result many still lie buried under what would become Cheesman Park. In 1909, the widow of prominent Denver businessman Walter S. Cheesman donated the Neoclassical Cheesman Pavilion.

Sunken Garden Park, part of Mayor Speer's City Beautiful initiative, is located at 8th Avenue and Elati Street in front of West High School. The park was completed in 1907 and the school was built in 1925. Both are still in use today.

The A & B Block faces the busy intersection of Curtis and 17th streets. The Isis Theater is on Curtis. A man on the right takes a drink from a public drinking fountain.

A crowd gathers in front of the Denver Post building located on Champa Street. They are listening to a man give a play-by-play of the 1927 World Series from a balcony on the building. He uses three large megaphones. An electric scoreboard mounted on the wall behind the man posts the score and the game's statistics.

A Denver traffic officer stands in the tramway boarding zone and stops traffic on 16th Street. The Daniels and Fisher Tower is visible in the distance.

Lita Grey Chaplin, an actress and Charlie Chaplin's second wife, sits in an open two-seater plane at Denver Union Airport.

Photographer William L. Ford stands on the corner of 16th Street downtown. A man in a boater looks through the viewfinder.

Customers crowd the entrance to the Golden Eagle Dry Goods Company department store, located at 16th and Lawrence streets, following a robbery in May 1931. Signs and banners on the building advertise a $100,000 markdown sale.

In this image spectators view bi-wing aircraft of the Denver Municipal Squadron of the Colorado National Guard at the Denver municipal airport.

In this view of 16th Street the signs for two of Denver's most famous movie theaters are visible, the Denver and the Paramount.

Colorado Governor Edwin C. Johnson stands at a radio microphone with University of Colorado football star Byron "Whizzer" R. White at his side. During his career, Byron R. White was a Rhodes scholar, played professional football for the Pittsburgh Steelers and the Detroit Lions, and served as a United States Supreme Court Justice for 31 years.

People pose in Echo Lake Park, one of Denver's mountain parks. Mount Evans, one of Colorado's "fourteeners," is visible in the distance.

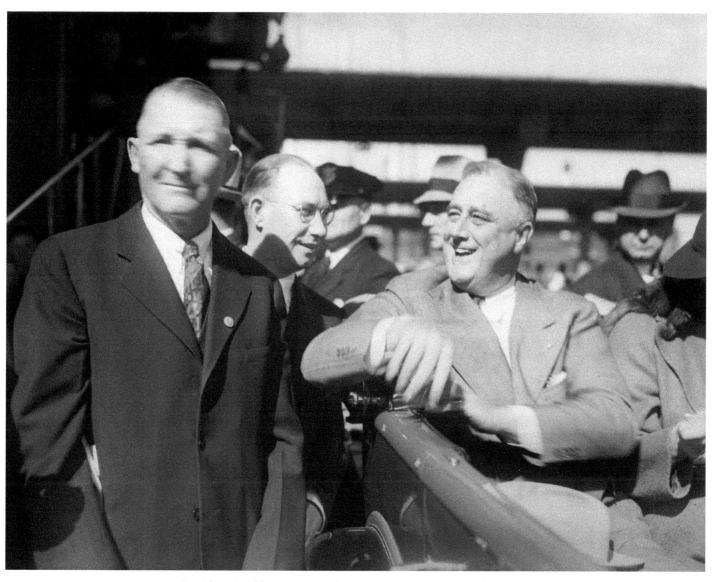

President Franklin D. Roosevelt sits in an open touring car during a campaign visit to Colorado in 1936.

Pedestrians crowd the sidewalks of 16th Street. The F. W. Woolworth Co. 5, 10, and 15 Cent Store is open for business at the corner of 16th and Champa streets. The store is located in the Symes building erected in 1905.

Here the Brown Palace Hotel stands on the corner of 17th and Broadway in the Central Business District, and the Midland Savings building is in the distance on the left. Bunting and banners that read "Welcome Rotary" hang over the street.

The Denver Fire Department fights a fire at the Colorado Wood Products Company, which was located in the 1200 block of Curtis Street.

THE WAR ERA

(1940s)

Pedestrians cross Stout Street in the Central Business District as two electric trolleybuses ply 16th Street. The Denver Tramway company trolleybuses were put in service in 1940.

A crowd watches the University of Denver Pioneer football team at the 30,000-seat stadium, which was located on the DU campus from 1927 to 1974. The football program was discontinued in 1960.

The Gano-Downs clothing company was an upscale men's store located on the corner of 16th and Stout. In the 1940s the company updated the building's facade to the moderne style.

The Barclay Block, located at 18th and Larimer, was built as a business block and later became hotel apartments. In the late 1940s and early 1950s, the building reflected the overall economic decline in lower downtown Denver.

Members of the Roundup Riders of the Rockies, a private organization made up of prominent Colorado business and professional men, pose near a United Airline's charter plane at Denver's Stapleton Airport. Every year the members make a trail ride over the Continental Divide. The organization has a foundation dedicated to trail creation and improvement.

The Daniels and Fisher Department Store was located on the corner of 16th and Arapahoe streets and completed in 1912. The department store was for many years one of the city's finest retail establishments. The business was later sold to the May Company and became the May–D&F Store. This building was closed and razed in the 1970s. The Daniels and Fisher Tower was also slated for destruction, but was saved by preservationists and still stands today.

By the late 1940s Larimer Street had many bars and flophouses.

Notes on the Photographs

These notes, listed by page number, attempt to include all aspects known of the photographs. Each of the photographs is identified by the page number, a title or description, photographer and collection, archive, and call or box number when applicable. Although every attempt was made to collect all data, in some cases complete data may have been unavailable due to the age and condition of some of the photographs and records.